In the Country of the Peregrine

In the Country of the Peregrine

Wade Stevenson

BlazeVOX[books]
Buffalo, New York

In the Country of the Peregrine
by Wade Stevenson

Published by BlazeVOX [books]

Printed in the United States of America

Interior design and typesetting by Geoffrey Gatza
Cover Art: Geoffrey Gatza

First Edition
ISBN: 978-1-60964-423-9
Library of Congress Control Number: 2022945501

BlazeVOX [books]
131 Euclid Ave
Kenmore, NY 14217
Editor@blazevox.org

publisher of weird little books

BlazeVOX [books]

blazevox.org

21 20 19 18 17 16 15 14 13 12 01 02 03 04 05 06 07 08 09 10 11

BlazeVOX

To Whom It Is Written
O lost and by the wind grieved, come back again

Table of Contents

In the Country of the Peregrine

Peregrine, Latin PEREGRINUS, is a name originally meaning "one from abroad", that is, a foreigner, a traveler, a pilgrim, one having a tendency to wander, not native to a region or country.

It may also refer to a bird of prey, a peregrine falcon.

THE SONG OF THE PEREGRINE

If you took time to steal a backward
Glance into the mirror of your memory
it may amaze, startle your mind to wonder
Who stole some essential part of you
From your deepest, your true blue you?
How you became a peregrine wanderer
Gyring in exiled flight, hunting
Your missing "me", primal homeland
Your own home bombed to shambles
Your country overrun, language lost
Waking up in an alien geography
To a different nuance of light
No surprise to realize you're just a digit
In that great unwritten book
Of all the nameless, placeless people

POEM FOR A PEREGRINE

I look back at my life, try to understand
Why the magic moments so quickly here
Then just as suddenly gone
Shouldn't it be easy to understand?
It wasn't just one failed memory
No, there were many, see how they slip
Shuffled backwards
In the two way mirror of time
Though I always knew
Looking into that other forward mirror
What was loved would continue to grow
But never come back
The end seeded with the beginning
With no promises given
Of what would happen after the end
Love, memory, sex, oblivion, desire
There were the bare bones
On which I tried to build my body
Then in the shadow of a tree
In a simple seam of dust
The house of love I longed to live in
Came crashing down beam by beam
The Amor I thought mine not truly my own
Long ago my Mama had warned me
A poet like you will never have a home

IN A TREACHEROUS TIME

In a treacherous time there was a tortuous love
I followed a path that led from my lips to your eyes
I was full of lonesome and lonesome longing for love
I let myself be loved until I was truly —
No end to those nights of a momentary Amor —
If you'd asked me to make love
Inverted on my head I would have tried
You led me into a darkness darker than I had known
With sweet words taught me how to play games
From backwards to forwards then back again
Then once again up and down hill all over again
We both knew the end would come
When it did —
It was the most treacherous ending of all

SURVIVAL IS AN ART

Survival is an art
(I repeat to myself)
Every day I try long and hard
To play my assigned part
But it doesn't work —
Whatever I was born for
I can tell you one thing
I goddamn never got
And that's a fucking fact
So tomorrow once again
I'll clamp on my made-up mask
Do my best to improve my act
It's true I tried for years
To urge my heart to stop
Since it seems I'm condemned to live
I'll just go on stumbling, trembling, tumbling
One thing for sure —
I won't look back

MY BODY POEM

In the body
By the body
Of the body
For the body
To be the body
Only the body
Nothing but the body
To be embodied
In the body in the breath
That comes from the body
In the flesh that is the body
To live breath, body, mind
All at once, past, present, future
Embodied or disembodied
In the brief convulsive beauty
Of this body which is mine
Before I go
I just want to do it good
One last time

IN REMEMBRANCE OF OUR MOMENTS

Moment by memorable moment
To moment each moment—
Across unlived gaps of nothing —
At the edge of the cliff of non-being
Before the decisive act occurs
Every moment shapeshifting
Into the next so that one moment
Is never precisely the same
As the remembrance of one before
Coupled with desire for the after
Ceaselessly becoming itself again
Moment to moment by musical moment
Until the last moment when all the moments
Run out of the moments they birthed
The momentum of all our special moments
    Madly lived/ fleetingly fulfilled
    Achingly loved/ memories revived
Morph into one monumental moment
Made of all the momentary moment by moments
    What you have just lived: your life

YOU, HERE

Can you turn blue inside out?
Or turn the sky upside down?
Can you measure the distance between a thumb
The real print of your peregrine heart?
Don't you know behind the highest power Amor
Are hidden tens
Of angry grinning ghosts?
The silence of the darkness is deafening
The night clairvoyant
You can see so much of what once you didn't know
That you could almost die for the knowing
Why is it that darkness always exceeds the light
As loss acts as a solvent
Washing away all the attempts at love?
What have you got when you've got no more to give?
And the world only contains one object
Which is YOU — a naked being standing here
Head tilted toward the blackening sky
Hemmed in by everything you didn't do
A certain sweet tenderness of no real use
In your lifelong tussling match with moments
Always migrating into minutes, into hours
All of them drifting away, bubbles of air

FROM THE BED OF MEMORY

Let the chandeliers be lit
Let all the candles blaze
Above the bed of memory
Where the phantoms of lost loves sleep
But it's so dark inside the body
Strange how even after you've loved so much
No light remains
There is no memory in the hip bones
One day you'll find another home
Where you always knew you belonged
The miracle of the flesh will again come alive
The tenderness you knew will be your dwelling
There will be no more fear or absence
The night will shine like the sun
The phantoms will rise from the bed of memory
And waltz again in the light

MY ZIPPERED LIPS

I won't tell you where I've been
What I've done or whom I've loved
I'll just keep my mouth shut
I won't say a word
I will never reveal
What is too painful to remember
Yet too hard to try to conceal
Kidnapped by my father
Forced to live in a world I didn't want
Cast aside by my mother
Who paralyzed couldn't have helped
Had she tried or even wanted
There was no way out
I simply fell apart
It took a long time
Before all my missing molecules
Snapped back into place
There was no "milk of human kindness"
I only came to know the taste of blood
In a lonely cell of fear and solitude
Out of that stone darkness
I clawed my way back
But I'll never tell you
The bitch of what I had to do,
How much I had to live, how much I lost

OLD MAN ME

There's a box on my shoulders
Inside sits a head
There are two eyes that ask
Do you know how to read?
There's a tongue that has forgotten
The language of love
It once knew how to talk
And what about the nose?
Frozen in time —
It can't forget to remember
All the scents of the past
If only the body could speak —
This is one promise it will never keep:
I will only get better in time
Amazing how along the edges of the mind
There still insistently stings
The stiletto blade of desire
A shiver of hope uncoils like a snake
In the bruised core of an old man's soul

THE SPARK OF THE HEART

I will take you now, I will take you tomorrow, I will
Always take you, I will keep you with me and take you again
To the secret place where the swallowtails go
You will laugh and come and we will find the table
Where the banquet has already been prepared
In the kingdom of Amor it will be the best of times
No need for words or stupid poetry rhymes
My kiss on your lips will mark the certainty
Together we will write the book of man and woman
Ripping up the pages as soon as we are done
Of what we were as lovers nothing will remain
Except the spark of a heart, a sudden lift in the air

BORN TO DIE

I'm told I was born naked
But I don't want to die naked
I want to die nude
In a warm place for a homeless heart
My body stretched out
Startling cartography
Of all the loves I ever had
In the pure nudity
Of my wrinkled naked body
There will be no shame
The phantoms of lovers past —
I can count them by the tens —
Surrounding me like a halo
In the Byzantine gold of that love
You can feel a faint echo
A remembrance of what we knew
While we lived and were alive
Letting all our Amor
Sweetly savage our skin

WOULD IT MAKE A DIFFERENCE?

Would it make a difference
If you found a word for the wind —
A word for all the things you loved —
The way on a certain summer evening
The light lingers in the amethyst air
And wouldn't it be interesting if —
For the solitude or a human face
You could find a simple way
To make the accumulated pain escape
The dark-eyed stare of living loss
For that you need words that leave a trace
A mark engraved, a rose tattoo
Before, wavering, they disappear
Submerged in the wake of a dwindling day

IN THE COUNTRY OF THE PEREGRINE

On the cusp of this cruel and tender world
Let me die content
Who knows why I was born without a nest?
I knew from the beginning
With the blood knowledge of the badly born
I belonged to the vast country of the wandering
The exiled, the too early departed
I became a nomadic lion homesick for a cage
An angry bee fighting for honey in a hive
A hungry dog prowling solitary streets
I lost my head for a love without reason
I'm tired of that furor and this frenzy
To try to go back would be spiritual treason
It's time to dig down deep in the dirt
Find a real home there
Kissed by the earth

SSHHH!

SSHHH! Be quiet, it's time to follow
The trapline
That leads the wandering bee
To fragrant flower
You in your forlorn hole
Your exiled hollow
Also long to become a waveform
Or vibrant hum
Make me new, make me naked
Make me one with you
Time dissolved in deepening shadows
Transported, transfixed
At last you understand the true nature of
A peregrine Amor
How swooping down swiftly from
Both above and below
There's no limit to love, life's vertical flow

HERE COMES THE SUN

If my body could speak
If only it could find the words to express
What escapes the language snare
Think of how much it would have to say
Speak, body, tell me all you've come to know
The long painful wisdom acquired
Through tens of days, nights, years
Tell me all you didn't ever want to know
The sudden ache of an impaled surrender
The dripdrip torture of a remembered rape
If memory had a key you'd simply press "delete"
What the body knows or can't forget
Is more than hard to find the words to say
If language had a body the mind could touch
It might simply utter "fuck"
Strange how four Anglo-Saxon letters
Contain the most powerful meaning
But here's the secret promise, the real thing
One day soon in one
Illumined moment of your plundered life
A sublime Amor will come to heal
All those ancient fucking wounds

I LIVED SO CLOSE

I lived so very close to my life
Sometimes it seemed my life and I were one
Joined at the hip rather than split at the spine
I think of the poet who said: *You must change your life*
So many times I tried to move
                    Into a difference space
I tricked myself into believing I could follow
                    The Way, the Truth, the Life
My own cracks, fissures, gaps finally shunted
                    Me off that well-worn track
I bent down, I bowed my head, accepted my fate
                    Let the world's will be done
                    Let the karmic knife come down
So what if all that happens is I lose my head?
I've always been in love with the lost
                    The broken, the uprooted
I let it all go down, kept on running until I found
                    The wounded fruit of a forever Amor

TO MY PEREGRINE LOVER

Give me one moment —
From the darkness of birth
A lucky spin among billions —
When chance and choice converge
For our bodies to cohere
We'll make it sublime
Caught in transit —
A convulsive tremor in time —
Free flying, flying high
As the flash of the flight
Of the peregrine soaring
On the solar winds of Amor

WHAT THE CROW KNOWS

It's funny when I think of you my words go transparent
You see right through them as if they were made of glass
I'm a poet and I use words to fight the world
But when you became my world
The words dissolved in you
Tens of days went by when I lived without a word
In the silence of the not-said the body understood
Though I never stopped trying to find a word for you
There was a black crow on a dark tree going *Caw Caw*
I heard lying next to your curving in a state of awe
I finally found a word so raw
Like a sliced open still beating heart
Outside the window on the shadow tree
The black bird with the diamond eye crowed
The word I found I polished till it shined
It was pure Amor and I knew then you were mine

SONG OF THE PEREGRINE MAN

A solitary man
His solitude holds him up
            As water a cork
            As a pine branch snow
A police siren wails
Someone else somewhere again
            Has failed
The solitary man walks alone
If the skyline were to topple
He would go on like a ghost
Stumbling through the rubble
He's amputated the past
Exchanged any promise of a future
For a permanent nomadic moment
            In a death-defying now
He's a filigree figure, an isolated
            Giacometti man
I'm sure you know the theme
Of the two songs he silently sings
About the blackness of the sun
Dynamite brightness of the lunar night

IN THE SUMMER SOLSTICE

In the summer solstice of my life
Under the strawberry moon of June
When the winter skeletons of trees
Know it's time to parade their green leaves
There will be no more loss of love
No death of an earth-bound desire
We follow the old ancestral urge and rise
In silence to the limit of that verge
Where the blue water reflects an ocean sky
The history of where we were or who we are
Falls away in a lengthening curve
That extends to the edges of time
Everything once loved will return again
The corn stalks will wave in green fields
The sunflowers will shine in the night
Our bodies joyfully joined
In the pull of the flow, the float of the stream
Of what when the final cataclysm comes
Will be remembered as no more than a dream

THINK ABOUT IT

Think about it
What makes you who you are
Not someone else?
It would be so easy to be someone else
It's the same breath that breathes
The same heart that beats
The same blood that flows
Right now you're glued to yourself
Wouldn't it be a welcome move
To be time-shifted into the non-binary
Body of someone else?
It would be like hitching a ride
On a different train
To a nowhere destination
That nonetheless when you get there
Will always be the same
This is how it would go
If you're white you could be black
Multicolor, brown or beige
A cloud in the sky
A feather dancing in the breeze
It's all part of a slight twist
Of optics, a brief change of scene
You could choose to give or to receive
Be a man, a woman, or an in-between
Anything at all
Whatever you goddamn please

IN MEMORIAM OUR WILD DAYS

Once we were more than wild
This is how wildly we lived our only life —
It *wilded* us. It was wild before us
Then when we lived it
It became wild again
If someone had to do wild
It was only right for it to be us
We got back to our essential God-
Seeded nature, wild and wilder
In both body and mind
Wilding to such a degree
You might have thought our wildness
Would have crashed and crushed us
At the end but for a change
We grew beyond the wild animals
That we were, throwing
Caution to the wind, with the light
Of our bodies we broke out
Of the darkness that sometimes dwelled
In our souls, we were wild, we were young
No matter how — we wildered and won

TELL ME WHAT IT'S FOR

Tell me what it's for
Is it the whisper of a flicker
Or of a full-fledged flame?
Is there an after or before?
Does it even have a name?
Should I be deeply angered
Or just mildly amused?
Please tell me — I need to know —
What the fuck is it all for?
Is there a meaning to this madness?
A reason to the rhythm
Of the dumbly revolving seasons?
Please tell me — before I die —
There's one thing I absolutely —
Before continuing the absurdity —
Strange how a life can depend
On such a simple single thing
As needing wanting to know
What the hell it all was for?
That question that holds me back
The very echo of my words
Burning in the back of my head
Prevents me from going to —
Blindly I must keep going on
Being born… being born…

YOUR ORANGE, YOUR LIFE

Your life —
Squeeze it
Like an orange
Suck the
Juice
Then eat
The peel
Inhabit
The inner glow
The real solar feel

STAYING ALIVE

I'm trying to keep myself alive
Carefully I sidestep the soap
That slipped between my hands
On the floor of the shower
It's not so easy to keep the spirit alive
When the semaphore body
Keeps flashing signs
That it is more than ready, eager to go
But I think the time at last has come
To unwrap all the dark
Secrets long buried in my mind
I'll tell you I love you in French
I'll break all the old bottles of wine
Although I can no longer speak
I'll do my best to make you laugh
No need to worry, my dear
Even though I'm six under
The grass will continue to green
Under your delicate feet
The body you loved will in time
Become water as it always does
At least my scraggly hair will be washed!
You who are destined to remain
Please make sure you tell the true story —
Even in hellish depths of the tundra season
How I loved beyond logic or reason

IN THE DARKNESS OF THE AUTUMN

In the darkness of the autumn or is it rather
In the autumn of the darkness
One man one lonely face —- was it me?
Was it some other version of myself
In the dark house of the autumn
Or was it someone else claiming to be me?
Another poor human being lost in the darkness
Of autumn. What if the darkness
Were a door, behind the door a light
That solitary man in the darkness
Of autumn had dreamed about the light
Because he knew the light was always there
He didn't know behind which door
In the quiet coolness of the autumn darkness
The man who claimed to be me
Who was someone other than the "he"
I thought I once knew
Had only one thing left to do —
He started walking toward

AND GOD SAID

Let there be he
Let there be she
Let there be he and she together
Let there be a he-she
One body united, indivisible
Let it not be a heresy
If a he is not really a he
And if a she is not truly she
If the he-she wonderful thing
Is like a legend told through time
If there never was a real he
If there never was a purely she
But if he were always part of she
As she were always part of he
So that individually and together
They were each a he-she
One sex containing the sex of the other
Merged and fulfilled in peace
No more need for a separate WC!

THE PALACE OF THE PURPLE ROSE

I seek the palace of the purple rose
There, in the uncreated darkness
A phallic flame flickers and glows
This is where desire becomes devotion
A gift, a cosmic dedication
On the mythic wall of that sublime emotion
Decipher the cryptic inscription
Above a man and woman naked
A red arrow welded through their hearts
Knowing is loving
To love is to know
To know is to love
That is all you ever need to know

BREATHING WITH YOU

I'm inches away from what I want
Tens away from what I need
Or is it the other way around?
How can I be so close but so far
Grounded earth deep
Yet capable of flying so high?
I may be inches away from a face
Tens from a body I long to fuck
I can almost touch your breath
As inches away I listen to you breathe
If I breathe slowly in and out
All the while remembering
I'm inches away from what I want
Miles away from what I need
If only longing and being could become one!
I'll go on breathing with your breath
Listening for every long inhale in, exhale out
Breathing together with you
Lying tethered/untethered to you
Close but still so far
I humbly ask you for just one thing:
Please don't ever stop

GOING TO THE SUN

I have a fragile sense
I'm approaching the western sun
I've lived my life in shifting zones
In variegated, violent, overlapping
Intermingled patterns of darkness and light
Now I ask: please let me go to the sun
I promise I'll spread myself out
Like a woman in love
In ghostly rooms of golden light
So let the beautiful body break
I will be pain-pure, loss released
Feeling not even the most remote hurt
Because I don't live there anymore
All the liquid loves I left —
The gut longings not fulfilled —
Will simply fall away from me
Like leaves from tired trees
Wade will no longer have to wander
He will just lap away like a wave
Wrapped in a haze
Of the deepest royal blue
In search of the unknowable yonder

THE HOUSE WE LIVED IN

The house we lived in is empty of all
A band of vagrant sorrows has moved in
Who is going to clear the space?
The past, the pain, the loves, the voices?
You were my royal You-ness
To which I added my humble me-ness
Creating a vital connectedness
Whirling cosmic energies reflected
Bodies of clay and bone resurrected
We were hieroglyphed, scratched, scrawled
Upon the stone surface of days, into years
Snapshotted in time like a truck laden
With the sparkling gasoline of diamonds
On the scars of heavenly highways
For one beautiful instant we were sign
Word and image conjoined
The outside shape matched the inside form
Conflicts resolved, losses absolved
This love born the new norm
Out of energy caught, transformed
Shifting nebulae, novae of light
Appeared suddenly, a solitary flare
Our matchless love burning match

YOU, ALWAYS

Here it comes again
That time-flavored, life-ripened feeling
Something started, something flew past
I know I'm almost at the end
But right up to that red line
Long before the end could become the end
I also knew it had to be you
It was always you
Your solar face, lunar blue eyes
Your sex you lovingly made mine
It was never anyone else but you
It's true I loved you without knowing
Who you truly were
I touched without looking
Touched with my eyes
Looked with my hands
Fucked with a far-flung feeling
Your identity a secret, a multiplicity
Hidden on a path that diverged
Toward a new version of corporeality
One and one is not just one
But it's not two either
When I'm tens into you
We breach beyond the boundaries

In that magnetic field of love
No more solitary, no more binary
You, my first heart throb
Very simply robbed my heart
Entranced in a trance
A never-ending open-ended
Sexual dance, sensually wild romance
Because you knew this too would die

Because you sensed what
A sublime Amor could be
Always the touchless ecstasy
Almost as easy
As this last in and out breathing

TO THE AMOR OF THE SUN

Rising fresh
Over the lawn of a new dawn
Comes the love of an older sun
No need to worry
What is hidden beneath
What might go beyond
Or perhaps was left behind
By another night's passing
Enjoy the ephemeral gold
Of one morning unfolding
Over today's freshly cut grass

FOR UKRAINE

The hospital buildings razed
Streets uprooted like trees
The air smoking under the weight of the dust
From ruins of the rubble and the doom
Of all the death
Ghosts of dead bodies
Women and children rise
Close your eyes, you will see them
Silhouetted against a dawning sky
Dancing with angels

KILLING THE WOLF

The body's inner shadows leave no trace
But if you search carefully
In one angle of the hidden recesses
You will find the pawprints of a wolf
  That wild wolf was me
He was hungry for the meat of all
  The memories of my life
I had to fight him tooth to tooth
  Me against me
The bitter struggle to find the truth
Of whether in my better days there was ever
  A hint of blue sky
When the wolf is done he stares at me
  Wolf eyes burning in the night
All the remembrances my little life had captured
The water the grass the light your curves my love —
  The reminiscences that refuse to fail —
  You are dying, the wolf warned
The blood you have now is not the blood that was
  I don't want to ruin the rest of your life
But the time has come to forget the glorious
  Of all the Amor and more you lived before
  There is no need to feel loss or sadness
You lived to the overflowing edge the life you had
  The love you shared is all you've got
I put a blindfold around my head and with a revolver
In my hands I blindly shot the wolf straight between the eyes

WHAT WILL YOU DO?

What will you do when it comes
When the decisive moment is almost here
Have you the force to live fully your final act?
Will you turn your head away in disbelief?
Or will you lift your arms, try to push back
The dull dark shadows invading your head?
What I want is to feel it intensely
As if it were an orgasm, a sacred act of love
I want to quickly roll all my memories into a ball
To be buried in the earth, like a precious scroll
It will be too late to try to rearrange
All the missing jagged pieces of a broken life
No second chances. The weight of what was
Will crush the promises of what is to come.
You won't have to worry about waking up
At five to six hungering for the sun to break
As you adjust the pillow under your restless head
You had a lifetime to make up your story
Tens of years may go by before you're born again
So just relax. It's time to lie quiet, be very still
Until she whom you at last have learned to love
Comes and with a cool damp cloth
Gently closes your baby blue eyes

A TALL TALE FOR Y'ALL

This is a tale almost too tall to tell
A logical mind might disbelieve
But it's the fundamental connection
Primordial interconnectedness
Of the all to the All
Beyond any repair
Or possible recall
No holds barred
From the ant to the plant
The snail to the star
From the elusive subatomic
To the exploding supra cosmic
That makes it possible for you
To even be here for a moment at all
Y'all

KNOWING THE NOW

The Now is here
Now you see it
Now you don't
Tantalizingly close
Unreachably far
Impossible to know
It lives to die
And dies to live
Vanishing
In its own becoming
It has no density
Always collapsing on itself
Renewed, reborn, unique
Indivisible, irrecoverable
So here it comes again
The ticking timebomb
Of the eternal Now
See if you can catch it
Before it explodes in your face

MY FIRST FIGHT

It was a long hard fight
Clear from the first shuddering
Contraction that I absolutely
Had no desire to come out
Dr. Mellon had to squeeze
My egg of a pincered head
But if I was going to die
Into the unforgiving light
Of an already wasted world
It had to be naked feet first
They washed a bawling body like a sack
My pink penis already cloaked in color
No peace to the mental stress
Of wondering how the brutal extraction
Would lead to a higher Amor reaction
How this piece of wrinkled flesh
Swarming alive with protoplasmic neurons
Would ever rise above the exquisite corpse
Of life's long impatient delay
At an amazing velocity of thought
To begin once again the cosmic play:
My very own, my one and only

ABOUT WADE

Before I was born Wade
I was a wave
A wave afloat in a vast amniotic sea
I was a wave in the morning, a wave at night
A sweet tender blue wave at twilight
I wanted wave to be my name
In the warm maternal magic fluids
I could continue to waver and flow
I never wanted to be a Wade
Better to be a nameless one
Unborn, watching the waters rise
The waves endlessly breaking
My special wave cresting, peaking
Speeding mercilessly toward the shore
Toward life and light
Through my mother's bloody
Wide open pelvic door
So it was and was no doubt meant to be
How a tiny blue wave rippled and rose
Became a man, now old, named Wade
Amazingly like me

I HAVE LOVED SO MUCH

This is how the long absence of your absence begins
Before the darkness shone, after the stars crashed
So difficult to finesse that finest of lines
Between the moment when you are here
The other moment when you are no longer there
From here to there it's all over in a match flash
How could it possibly happen?
Suddenly going absent to your own life
Observing from afar in panic wonder
How even the smallest fragments of what you loved
Fall away, splintering
There is no light in that darkness
You'll never even come to a basic understanding
Of how you came to be at all
From a zygote to a complex web of consciousness
You finally found a word to cling to
As you walked down the long last sentence
It was what you had come from
What you always knew you had come for
When the night was the darkest, blackest
You remembered the first and last word *Amor*
Love transformed into light
The darkness shone
It will be easier to say goodbye
When you can simply say
I have loved so much

MY FUCKING LIFE

My fucking life
Is such a futile flash
It flares, flames, goes
Quick as the scratch
Of a match
The only witness of my Amor
Consumed in the ash

WHAT COMES AFTER?

When you wonder about what comes after
At the end of your long soul-thirsty journey
Is when you painfully start to remember
Everything that came before
The day we ran naked in the rain
Holding hands, laughed
At the silence of the birch tree forest
Or in Paris when you bathed with cubes of ice
Seeking to defeat the August heat
The vast unknown space of the after
Is soon defined by the intensity of the before
The invisible weight of a lover's body
Pressing down deeply
On the full length of your mind
If I could just hold on a little longer
Keep the exact feeling intact
The way the sun has of striking a wall
In the late afternoon
Or the way you sat astride a stone ledge
Slowly disrobing an orange
A few peels on the ground catching the light
Cheers! Here's to a long and full after
So you can better suck out the essence
Of everything lived, loved, lost before

FROM NOTHING TO SOMETHING

How can nothing become something
Something mutate into nothing again?
A memory of love searching for a self
Or a naked brain wiped clean?
Is a nothing really nothing?
Is a something more than something?
Or are nothing and something essentially one?
If you had to choose
Between something and nothing
Knowing each are interchangeable
Which would you choose first?
Imagine if from the grass roots of nothing
An exotic flower of something would blaze
Even when nothing fills the mental space
Something is always arising
From nothing to something and back again
Round and round we randomly go
Where, when, or how the memories stop
We will never really know
Suppose nothing became darkness
Something cloned into light
Then endless patterns of light/darkness
Would alternate, co-mingling, merge
We could take something from nothing
Or turn something back into nothing
Until the day when a Sun Amor is born
A new light will burn in the darkness
There will be no more nothing
An eternal kingdom of a sacred something

BEING AND BECOMING

I'm so tired of being
I just want to become
How do I transition from the stasis
Of the humdrum everyday being who's me
To the promise of forward movement
Of an infinitely possible becoming?
If I could find a simple way
To put a decisive end to a limited life
The funeral procession of similar nights
Revolving into identical days
With a fresh fledged body, open green mind
I would joyfully test the waters
Leap into the sea of becoming
Become one with the happening waves
Caught between my fear of non-being
My lust to become, I have to break down
The walls that keep me from falling
If I could just jump out of my being —
 A narrow escape —
Merge with the wild wave of becoming
Riding that wave on the wind of tomorrow
I would gladly give up my name
Kill the ego, slay that tired old game
I don't want to be who I am anymore
I'm absolutely dying to become
To touch the future of my body
To learn the love that will haunt
My whole corporeal being
No more living only on hope
Slashing the throat of the quotidian habit
I'll reveal the God of my dreams
The promise of an infinite becoming
My newly born paradise to be

FORGET IT

Forget what you did
Forget what you didn't do
Forget everything
It's easier that way
Dying I mean
Because forgetting is just another way of dying
Letting the memories slide slowly away
One by one like boulders into the sea
It's quicker to forget and wonderful
How it triggers an almost orgasmic relief
From the pain of remembering
What you did or didn't do
What you tried to love but could never have
Let them go piece by broken piece
All the feelingly felt, intimate emotions
Ripples in the wind, petals blown across the sand
Nothing to write, taste the freedom
From the hunger to recall
All the memories lived, loved, survived
Now merge into one memory monument
The cosmic mind of your conscious life
You must learn to forget
If you ever want to be free

MOMENTO MORI

What happens when at the end you're hooked
Inside the deep of your head
You don't feel anything, you flounder around
You're almost dead
Nothing is happening
But you're paralyzed with fear
You just want to open your mouth
And scream
You want to feel, fuck, love
You're suddenly alone
You're beginning to freak out
And it's getting worse
You've become a life-time prisoner
Of your corporeality
The brutal reality of your dying machine
If you could hang your throat
Cut your breath
You might be able to break your body
Your spirit would soar
Guess what: you're finally free!

AT THE END OF MY BREATH

What is there between you and me?
Is it more than one breath?
Perhaps even more than one life?
If we breathe
We can breathe together
In the in and in the out
Of our breathless movement
It's possible we become
Just one inhaled/exhaled breath
No more than that between us
One long deep heart breath away
From being never apart
To be born is to breathe
We rise on the breath
We die on the breath
You will always be one with me
In the presence of my breath
In the absence of my breath
When I can no longer breathe

A FAREWELL TO WORDS

I write: it's true
Because on the other side of me
Just beyond that obscure edge that separates
Life from darkness, just like the moon
Death is always rising
I tricked myself thinking my poems might save me
From the ultimate end of my little story
I soon found words are not the answer
They keep chasing, coupling with each other
Long after the last sentence ends
One word leads to, engenders another
If you added all the pages together
In time it would create a biblical book of absence
But life does not go on searching for a synonym
Or at least a rhyme. It comes to a sudden stop
Period. The End. Let it be done
Because the words can only scar the surface
Of what lies hidden in the life-blood story
No more poems, songs or lyrical lullabies
You have just read what I wrote with the pain
Of my bare hands: these ink-darkened pages
Do me a final favor, take them, tear them apart
Let all the ripped paper pieces of my life rise
Into the air, fluttering free

IN THE GARDEN OF THE OVERNIGHT WORDS

The first thing I do each morning when I rise
Is check my poems: did they survive the night?
Together/separately did they grow all right?
Did one letter learn to love the other?
Was a mere comma enough to pause them apart?
Do they need the spring rain of new-born words
To fertilize the secret souls sleeping
Under the ground of consonants and vowels?
Is the last sentence enough to seal their fate?
Should I add mushrooms to the language soil?
My words in time when they decay and rot
Birth a richer resonance, a finer-tuned assonance
I'll be the gardener of my past
Tirelessly sowing the seeds of sundered
Loves, composted memories
In the mulched earth of my own vocabulary
These words though written in a sun-struck room
Are all about my future decline, my on-hold doom
If death is the last flower of love
Love is the bloom that crowns the last goodbye

THE ACHING

I'm aching for the planet
I'm aching for the horror
Of all the on and on and on killing
I'm aching for the end
Of this sublime end-time game
Let's bow in reverent homage
To what we are
While we mourn together
For what we know now
We no longer will be
Before I go let me tell you
A little something about me
I'm a composite composition
Made up of dinosaur desires
Moon-injected fantasies
Like you I live poised on a pinpoint
Of nonexistent time
In an unresolvable way
Separated in my cell solitude
Yet entangled in the deepest love
At least my body is biodegradable
If only I could burn these bones
Let the flames take
What the fire in me always wanted
Here's a better idea:
Stepping out from behind the mask
Of my flesh I'll turn
My aching bones
Into fertilizer for a new green garden
The big bump we call a thinking head
Ballast to a ghost floating body
I want to throw in a landfill
Let nature do the rest

Here's what I really want to know:
When I die what will I fruit into?
It will soon be over
The apocalyptic decomposition of all
Scraps of dying sunlight
Will shine on the fallen debris
A few rabbits will run, scrounging
For food under layers of brown dust

TAKE A CHANCE ON DEATH

I'll take a chance on you
Next time it will be better
It will be better for sure
So let's cut the cord
Cut out all the memory ties
The emotional umbilical crap
Cut away the geography
On this useless map
In a space-time geometry
That has no meaning any more
If love and death go together
Like peas in a pod or milk with honey
Then to live is to die and reversed
To die is to live and reversed
Dying we live, living we die
Death born in life, life in death
The two married together, inseparable
Apart so let's hope for the best
Roll the joy-and grief-loaded dice
It's how the universal game is played
Through tens of interconnected
Space-time body-mind years
Relax in the cosmic knowing
Sooner or surprise! Right now
You'll come out, newly reborn, just fine

POEM FOR FOUR WORDS

Love first
Die later

THE DARKNESS YOU LEAVE BEHIND

It's coming now, coming closer
Coming from afar, from tens of years away
Drawing nearer every day
What you've patiently been waiting for
Don't be afraid it says
This won't be the first time
This has happened before
Will happen again
Close your reddened eyes, listen closely
To the voices chanting sweet sad songs
In the echoing chambers of your head
Lift your arms up, try to touch
The ceiling of that lost love feeling
The distance between you and your past
Slowly starts to erode away
Everything longed for, lived, loved
Catches up with you, POW!
One incandescent burning moment of Now
You become the he or she less or more
Of who you really were or are
It was always there locked inside
Yes, you had the time of your life
Extracting the joy from the pain of each day
As if there were no more tomorrows
Please don't ruin it now
Turn inwards, play again the blue velvet
Music of lingering twilight hours
The heart relieved will open and breathe
The bombed-out craters, the gaping holes
Will go up in flames in the darkness
No longer yours, you're leaving behind

THE HURTING

Let's go back to the primordial wound
When the real hurting began
How it starts with the womb
The original fissure, the first crack
That let the light in
Neither you nor I were close to finding a path
We had no way of knowing
What would be the future of our face
The disastrous glory of our all too human fate
The wound then no more than a passing feeling
A vague unacknowledged sense of loss
Partly due to the pain of all the time perishing
The wound born at the beginning —
It didn't announce itself
It lay sleeping in the wind
The real wounds came later
When the first primal wars were fought
Face to face, tooth to tooth, wound to wound
Whatever fragment was able to survive —
Whatever brief, basic, brutal, bloody—
Once again it came back to us —
Two lovers engulfed in the storm —
To find a voice for all the sutured
A prayer for the placeless, poem for the lost

BIRTHING POEM

Had I a gun
        I'd kill my past
Strangle its neck
        Before it kills me
I had waited for nine in darkness
The mind growing numb
How did I know already at birth
        To be born is to die
To crown close to the truth?
No use sucking my thumb
        Your birthday becomes
The day of your first departure
        If only I had a gun
It was already clear
        As I was pulled with a scream
Into the panic pain of the sun
All those promises my Mama made
Weren't going to be so much fun
        I decorated the blank book
Of the rest of my desperate days
With sketches of unfulfillable dreams
With limitless man-woman yearnings
        With words, poems, prayers
I finally conquered the limits of birth
Found a home in the air and the earth

THE TRAUMA TRAP

Trapped in the trauma of the doing
Or of what was once done
That can never be forgiven/forgotten
It's time to acknowledge the truth —
No exit from the cyclic wheel of being
It goes round again and again
From disembodied bodies—
All the memories dismembered—
One birth is never enough
At the same time as you bleed
For what's coming, you can't stop hearing
All the lonely cries of the refugees
The body bearing witness to the losses
Carved, cut too deep in the flesh to die
The phantoms of the absent continue to rise
From the killing fields of the mind
This poem, like all poems, doomed to fail
It never can come close to expressing
The extremity of the pain endured
Running on empty now
Without even feeling the need for doing
Hunting for love in the wild, hoping for hope
Against hope, against logic, against
The promise of life— so much easier
Now just to let go, to let the flesh
Become undone, to join the swelling ranks
Of the broken, the displaced ones
Revealing at last the real you:
Your breakable self, your love-shattered you

POEM FOR A NOMAD MAN

Please teach me the right way to be me
In my locked down life
The solitary vault
Of a soundproof mind
Reviewing fast forward images
Of all my squandered time
It's sad to say:
There's nothing more!
I live with a masked face
A body my complete lack of faith
Has finally painted blue
You can envision me sitting back-
Wards on a blue chair in a blue room
My blue body naked in a blue dusk
It would all be true!
So please forgive me for
Being no more than the man that I am
A nomad in transit, one more tenant in time

A HOMELESS HAWK SEEKS THE SUN

We've wasted our lives waiting for the future to come
That stupid stubborn thing — it never does!
No use either trying to live life to the deepest
When the bottom is touched
Another death always revealed
What we tried to cling to didn't hold
The curious way the present has
Of obliterating the past
Worried about an afterlife?
The best way of dealing with it —-
Deeply understanding how the sunlight
Falls on a wall
Or a single calla lily shines
What makes it all so hard
There's this thing caught up inside us —
            A larger darker thing —
Like a head inside a head, body inside a body
A still small voice keeps asking
What is that big dangerous thing inside?
            Death inside life
            Life inside death
The mind has no mouth, the tongue can't talk
We have lived so long without a history
We must invent our own
While we wait for our real future to come
The healing rains to wash away all the blood
            But the pain still stings
Our violence keeps peeling away the earth
            Like an onion ring
We must forget what it is to be human
Rise above the sorrow of all our days
            In full flight
A homeless hawk wings its way toward the sun

WORDS FOR A SOLITARY WALL

If it's true I am no more no less
Than the nothing that I am
What is it possible to say about me?
What am I? If not a "me" concealed
Behind another more eternal 'I"
Coming from nothing, going to nothing
From depths where the lord of nothing reigns
Words tell all but my words are also a wall
Wearing my poor pound of flesh like a shield
Trusting in bone-blood passions to make
The little left of the nothing of my life
Purposefully real — listen, can you hear
The song floating in the air?
Since a long time it's already here
Invisible, untouchable, ungraspable
Awaiting my consent to make itself known —
It's pure Amor
Now at the ground zero of solitude
Not knowing which direction to turn
Because you never knew where you began
It's time to surrender to that higher altitude

ELEGY FOR

The body's torn
Life has flown
The future fled
The past is dead
Across the cratered earth
Only flames remain
All the days together
All the good times and again
There's no reliving the loss
Even the most beautiful journey
Must die in the end
May the ghosts of our joy be happy
May they elude the lure of longing
Remembering everything loved
We had to leave behind

WHY DO THE STARS?

Why do the stars have scars?
From this earth where we are
They look homesick from afar
For too many silvered nights
Even as they coldly glistened
They couldn't help but listen
To the full phases of the moon
Singing lonely lunar love tunes

ONE GOOD THING

The good thing about
A fractured heart
Is that
Once it's broken
Only the pieces can crack
The amor that aches
Is never coming back

LOVE LOST & FOUND

Where do the lost and found loves live?
          Returned/unreturned
It doesn't matter — over time
They all will finally find a home
          Buried deep
In the heart's blood bone

TOO LATE

It's too late to repair
Too late to regret
Too late for the loss
For the holding on tight
Too late to unlearn
What you never asked to know
Once you thought you had a chance
Before the first fatal glance
Might even have believed
You were one of a kind
But it was never promised to be
As a child you cried in your sleep
Ran away from that home on the beach
On bare bloody feet
Later disguised your hunger for love
On another body primed in sexual heat
Too late now for safety of a home
Your life cut off at the knees
You must walk the rest of the way alone

THE TARGET IS LOVE

Be my revolver
Hold steady my hand
Together we'll fire
One Amor-armored bullet
Bang!
A once in a lifetime shot
Life-enhancing bullseye
Straight through the head
Into the target of the heart

IT TAKES TIME

It takes time
Could happen in a flash
The real and the beautiful
Finally face to face
Achingly, life-changingly
The beautiful turning away from —
Becomes real, the real turning
Inward, becomes beautiful
As the imaginary meeting
Of a moon dog
With its human master

FLIP A COIN

This may or may not be
It might be, possibly could be
Certainly would be if it could
Who knows if it might?
Then again it might simply be
In a pure stasis of self being
With no other evidence
To prove it really is
Or possibly is not
Because as it was written
At the beginning
This may or may not be
The choice is yours
Just as your life may
Never be resolved
Until near the end when
You're no longer here nor there
In that labyrinth of being
Only you might find out
Who and where you truly are
What was real or merely ephemere
This is how it was
How it once came to be
Then again was not
So don't wait
The jig will soon be up
Or maybe not

THE SUN IN MY HEAD

I have the sun in my head
See how it expands
Beating against my skull
Leading me back to the time
Of the bullfrog picnic
That day when I crossed over
Into the land of easy
After checking it out I knew then I wanted
It to go on and on
Lifting me so high
Into an oceanic sky
Sunday afternoons of naked
Body blues
The ongoing predicament of
Too many beautiful days
All the little bits of a spanking good time
Explosive orgies of a bitter knowledge —
You're going to lose everything you ever loved
The happy haystacks ignited
That's the only condition in which you'll be allowed
To start your life all over again.

MINUTES OR MOMENTS?

Some say minutes
I prefer moments
It's true sometimes a minute may billow
Can expand long into hours
Eventually evolving into days
As the music of time floats by
Before accelerating into years
A lot can happen in a minute
But nothing like what can occur
In one momentous moment
While you are waiting for the minutes
To morph into hours
To fast forward into days chasing days
One mad moment of wild Amor
Can set years, months, minutes and more
On fire — like sunflowers, ablaze

MY BREATH IS NOT MINE

There is no "I" in the breath
In the eye of the moment
The whoosh of the birth
The breath that I breathe is not me
Was never mine
I come from a faraway place
It took me a lifetime just
To become equal to my face
I struggled like a lizard wounded
A she snake always watching
Poised to strike
It's time to turn the page
Fast forward on the bullet train
From the first station of birth
To that undiscovered country
Another lightning vision of satori
It would be so much easier if
You didn't balance on the boundary
Of no more, no *mas*, never again
          All the journeys ended
          Memories sabotaged
          The voices silent
Only a whisper remains
It shouldn't be difficult
To wear the ending well
          Just don't digress
          Or try to possess
          A camouflaged joy
Close your eyes, go easy now
It's how it was always supposed to be
Not glamorous for sure, in a strange way
          Almost perfect

A HOME AT LAST

In a space empty of all possible fullness
Above burned fields, the smoke snaking
Between blackened buildings
Bodies dug in the blood-soaked earth
While one last shock of light remains
Below broken castles in the sky
The last few peregrines have fled
What a relief to find
Caught like a prisoner bare-assed
Naked between one puny pinprick
Of time and a god-gapped eternity
Alone on the homeless turf
There's a final refuge for you —
A home in the heart of the Sun Amor

IN SEARCH OF THE LOST

I search for what I've lost
Explore the empty memory rooms
Spring flowers in the garden of love
Killed by an unpredictable frost
Even the trees wander like ghosts
I try to tap into their trunks
Seeking the honeycomb of time
How to shake off the powdered dust
All the years flittered unconsciously by
Look at me now — face to face
Full frontal nudity, I'm down
To my final skin
There's so much left to love
With my going I will not
So I repeat the simple words
Goodbye ocean, sky, trees
Close your eyes, let the body levitate
Into the light darkness
It's really easy, done so many times before
It's just a breeze

GOODBYE POEM

You were one of those who sought
                                        the ultimate boundaries
No shame in that. Because you always pushed on.
There were many places when stopping
                                        would have been nice.
You didn't.
In that way — because of your restlessness —
                                        you became relentless.
You faced the challenge of the white space.
You won. You moved into it. You strode
                                        through it.
Never were your subjugated. That's what
                                        set you apart.
Now
Let your aging body agonize
                                        in peace.
The end is here — flat, simple
                                        and dark.
Nothing to be afraid of really.
                                        Close your eyes.
Touch your fingertips one last time
                                        to the lips
Of she who was much loved. Go yourself.
In one star-blasted moment

                                        you're gone.

Hello again
The end becomes the beginning, I await
                                        the dawning

Praise for Wade Stevenson's *In the Country of the Peregrine*

"Wade Stevenson focuses on reimagining the known image--making foreign that which is familiar in the world of the poem. In this ambitious effort, we see the complexity of love and loss intertwined. In this musically adept collection, I've no doubt you'll find something to love and perhaps even "a last refuge for you.""

—Kyle McCcord, Author of *Reunion of the Good Weather Suicide Cult*

"In one of his final public statements, the poet Charles Olson avowed "I have lived with my body so long, it must *be* my soul." *In the Country of the Peregrine,* Wade Stevenson records, with dauntless candor and unfailing tenderness, the wanderings of all flesh towards the flesh that is its ultimate home, i.e. towards unity. It is wonderful to discover in these poems a companionship that is also in itself a kind of odyssey, replete with enchantments. This is a most welcoming book."

—Donald Revell

Like its titular bird of prey, *In the Country of the Peregrine* veers gracefully among its disparate pursuits, taking peregrination itself—wandering, displacement, diaspora—as characteristic of human life. All existence, Stevenson urges, is part of "an infinitely possible becoming," the self "a nomad in transit," caught up, therefore, in wanderings both psychic and spiritual, temporal and corporeal—even the body, in Stevenson's hands, is revealed to be "swarming alive with protoplasmic neurons." By turns arch and elegiac, playful and pensive, Stevenson brings us face-to-face with the terror of mortality, at the same time reminding us that death itself is merely one phase in the endless arc of the universe. "One day you'll find another home," he writes, "where you always knew you belonged." These poems feel like precisely such a home, possessed throughout of gorgeous sonic textures and propulsive rhythms, and urging us—insistently, impactfully—toward renewed reverence for the wanderings we are.

— Christopher Kempf

The wonderful poems in Wade Stevenson's *In the Country of the Peregrine* are deliberate in their looking back and looking into possibility. Without relying much on punctuation, his poems are not stapled to the page—instead, they leave only the essential and intensifying clarity of a life's winter years. Expertly controlled line breaks and with raw honesty, the poems balance aging and loss with the grainy purity of *Amor*, a state of mind as much as a physical place. Many of these images leave lasting echoes and ripples long after the last poem.

—Sean Singer

Wade Stevenson's *In the Country of the Peregrine* collapses the two meanings of "peregrine" that open the collection: this book both wanders the landscape of the heart and makes of it a meal. Stevenson's poems swoop and dash themselves against memory, pain, love, and sex, again and again striving toward the light of healing on the horizon but knowing that way lies treachery. This is a collection full of experience, of the first-hand, excruciating knowledge of "the blackness of the sun / The dynamite brightness of the lunar night."

— Rachel Abramowitz

Wade Stevenson is a poet unafraid of asking the most ambitious philosophical questions: What multiplicity is housed within language? What emotional, narrative, and metaphysical weight accrues around the words we use every day, those familiar signifiers we only thought we knew? As Stevenson teases out possible answers to these compelling questions, each line shimmers with "a different nuance of light." This is a stunning and memorable book.

—Kristina Marie Darling, author of *ANGEL OF THE NORTH* and *DAYLIGHT HAS ALREADY COME*

Your poems move through philosophy, thought and spiritual ambitions. You create a vortex of ideas that churn into moments and moments into a full life. This is really well done in the poem IN REMEMBRANCE OF OUR MOMENTS The energy is what I think of you and your poetry. As it is impossible to imagine our own deaths, only our own lives. From THE BED OF MEMORY here is another wonderful line "There is no memory in the hip bones." And a gold star for these lines in THE SUMMER SOLTICE "Everything once loved will return again / the corn stalks will wave in green fields / the sunflowers will shine in the night".

—Geoffrey Gatza, poet and publisher of BlazeVOX Books

In this collection a "wandering" poet gazes at the trajectory of his life. A peregrine is a species of falcon, but the word has multiple meanings, traveler, pilgrim, foreigner. Images of exile and dislocation haunt this volume's verses, which steal across the boundaries of language, landscape, and personal history. In the opening poem Stevenson invites himself to wonder "how you became a peregrine wanderer?" Poems like "In Memoriam Our Wild Days" and "Birthing Poem" look back on earlier times with nostalgia and regret. The poet is at his most endearing when the language is playful, as in "About Wade," which begins, "Before I was born Wade / I was a wave / A wave afloat in a vast amniotic sea / I was a wave in the morning, a wave at night/ A sweet tender blue wave at twilight / I wanted wave to be my name." Death is another country whose border seems to loom ever closer on the horizon. The best poems are the ones in which Stevenson approaches death with wryness and wonder, and there are several moments when readers will be happy to share deeper with him into the dark.

—KIRKUS REVIEWS

Wade Stevenson's newest collection, *In the Country of the Peregrine*, in part adheres to such an approach, but rather than strict cataloging, there is a lyrical and narrative thread of understanding, acceptance, and vulnerability found throughout these poems. While Stevenson's speaker might mourn that they are "just a digit / In that great unwritten book / Of all the nameless, placeless people," they acknowledge not only the value of everyday life, but the fact that in the end, love and happiness will always outshine regret and missed opportunities. Stevenson's keen observation of the past and his honest portrayal of the present add to an already accomplished and important oeuvre, and with page after page of such stunning observation, you will be comforted with the notion that when the curtains at last close, it "will be easier to say goodbye" because you too "*have loved so much.*"

—Esteban Rodríguez, author of *The Valley* and *Before the Earth Devours Us*

Wade Stevenson was born in NYC in 1945. Educated at St. Paul's School, he studied in Paris, and has travelled extensively throughout Asia. His first book, ICE CREAM PARLORS IN ASIA, was published in 1969, thanks to John Ashbery. BEDS (McCall Publishing Co.) became a poetry best seller. His memoir ONE TIME IN PARIS and his novel THE ELECTRIC AFFINITIES both received critical acclaim. He has published more than a dozen poetry books, including THE ABSENCE OF THE LOVED, SONGS OF THE SUN AMOR, and LOVE AT THE END.

Made in the USA
Middletown, DE
10 January 2023